With best wishes,
Bob Sargent

WALKING
IN
NEWNESS
OF LIFE
The Sacraments
of Initiation

Robert Sargent, STD

Ne'

D1365069

Cover design by Sharyn Banks
Book design by Lynn Else

Library of Congress Cataloging-in-Publication Data

Sargent, Robert, STD.
    Walking in newness of life : the sacraments of initiation / Robert Sargent.
        p. cm.
    ISBN 978-0-8091-4383-2 (alk. paper)
    1. Baptism—Catholic Church. 2. Confirmation—Catholic Church. 3. Lord's Supper—Catholic Church. I. Title.
    BX2205.S27 2007
    234'.161—dc22

                                                                2007006252

Published by Paulist Press
997 Macarthur Boulevard
Mahwah, New Jersey 07430

www.paulistpress.com

Printed and bound in the
United States of America

Contents

Dedication
To B.A.S.
For faith and sacraments shared

Introduction

The sacraments of initiation are baptism, confirmation, and the Eucharist (or thanksgiving). In the Orthodox liturgies these three are usually given together, even to infants.

Our understanding of the sacraments is based on our beliefs about Christ, the incarnate Word. Jesus himself as incarnate is a sacrament or visible sign of God's universal love for us. In the New Testament there was a growing understanding about Jesus, from Paul's resurrection focus on Jesus as the one "declared to be Son of God with power according to the spirit of holiness by his resurrection from the dead" (Rom 1:3–4), through the understandings of Mark, Matthew, and Luke, until this understanding of Jesus culminated in John's pre-existence Christology of the Word.

Even in the early centuries of Christianity, as it moved into the philosophical world of the Greeks, the early councils struggled to reach the insight of Jesus' being one person with both divine and human natures.

It can be very helpful for our understanding of the sacraments to turn to our beliefs about Christ's being one person with both a divine and human nature. Our beliefs about Christ carry over into our beliefs about the sacraments, for the sacraments too include material objects such as water, bread, wine, and oil. And at the same time they also contain a divine grace or presence within them. We can see then that the structure of the sacraments is modeled after Christ, the incarnate Son of God.

In fact the Christology of each of the Evangelists finds an echo in the sacraments. In Mark, after the Father calls Jesus his beloved Son at the baptism, Jesus there anointed by the Spirit, in a way similar to professional wrestlers of the day, goes out to confront evil in its various forms, such as temptation, illness, and lack of faith. This is one facet of what our Christian sacraments offer us.

Matthew's Jesus delivers five major discourses in a way that parallels him to Moses, so that Jesus is seen as the new teacher of a way to fullness of life. Such an insight to life and knowledge from Jesus is carried over into the bread of knowledge and the experience of the other life-giving sacraments.

The poet Dante called Luke's Gospel the Gospel of the gentleness of Christ, for in Luke more than elsewhere, when Jesus sees the needs and sufferings of those around him, he is "moved with compassion." In this way Luke's Jesus is a revelation of God's loving kindness. The sacraments continue this role of helping us experience the Lord's loving kindness.

Finally, the first half of John's Gospel narrates Jesus' seven revealing signs, such as the miracle at the wedding at Cana in which Jesus revealed "his glory," that is, the presence of God in him. Such a notion of God's presence is central to the essence of the sacraments, all of them, but especially their epitome, the Eucharist. Jesus' signs in John not only teach us about Jesus, but also have sacramental overtones.

Another key notion of the sacraments is the notion of "grace," or the gift communicated to us in the sacraments. We speak of God's bestowing or conferring "grace" through the sacraments. We need to touch on an understanding of grace as found in the New Testament, and especially in Paul.

The New Testament word for grace is *charis,* which has the meaning of graciousness or beauty. Paul likes to link the word *charis* with the word *chara,* or joy.

Sometimes the word *charis* means a freely performed saving act, such as in Ephesians, where we read "But God, who is rich in mercy, out of the great love with which he loved us even when we were dead through our trespasses, made us alive together with Christ—by grace you have been saved" (2:4–5); and "For by grace you have been saved through faith, and this is not your own doing; it is the gift of God" (2:8).

In other passages *charis* is a personal quality of God, his graciousness, a quality that is shared and given to us. For example, in Romans 5:1–2 where we read: "Therefore, since we are justified by faith, we have peace with God through our Lord Jesus Christ, through whom we have obtained access to this grace in which we stand; and we boast in our hope of sharing the glory of God." Here Paul speaks of the Father's grace or graciousness as if it were a bright sunlight we are now basking in, for we have been given the gift to "stand" or live in this light or new state of friendship with God as a new creation.

Intimately related to the notions of Christ and sacraments is the context in which we find the sacraments, the church. The unity of human and divine natures in Jesus gives us an insight into the makeup of the church. In the church we have elements that are divine in origin, that is, instituted by God, and we have elements that are very human. Church members and church leaders can be very human, and at times even very weak. But that does not negate the church's continuing to be the "place" where our grace and salvation are found.

There are many images that try to express some facets of what the gift of the church is. It is the "people of God," as emphasized by Vatican II, that is a broad and ecumenical way of viewing the church, and a way that goes beyond some of the shortcomings of individualism. The church is also the "body of Christ," as taught by St. Paul, and revived very helpfully by Pius XII, an image that stresses the relation of the members to each other, and in a very personal way to Christ himself.

In the New Testament the word for church is *ekklesia,* with its meaning of "calling forth" or as implied, a "calling together." This is the word the New Testament authors use for the Old Testament word *qahal,* which describes the community that God has called together. This image focuses on the initiative of God in freely and creatively calling his people into this "place" of salvation.

Both church and sacraments are structured after what we believe about Christ as both God and man. And so, of course, we cannot come to a full understanding of the sacraments unless we look on them in terms of their relationship to Christ and to the community of believers. When we speak of "sacraments of initiation," we are talking about a joining or going into the person of Jesus, as well as into the people he has called together to belong to himself and to each other.

For Reflection:

1. How do we relate our understanding of the sacraments to the Christology of Mark? Of Matthew? Of Luke? Of John?

2. What are the connections and similarities between the structure of the sacraments and the church?

CHAPTER ONE

The Roots of Baptism in the Bible and in Early Christian Writers

Baptism in the Bible

The Christian initiation rites in the early church were one unified liturgy, even though today we now classify them as three sacraments. And yet we still find indications in our baptismal rites that they are oriented toward the reception of the Eucharist, such as the anointing of the mouth and senses to "open" or prepare the person for gifts to come.

Not only did the early Christians make no ritual break in the initiation ceremonies, but they seldom if ever made such theological distinctions as those concerned with the proper effect or grace of each sacrament as a separate entity. This liturgical and theological unity of the initiation rites implies that the content and meaning of baptism and confirmation are included in an eminent way in the Eucharist, so that each repeated reception of the Eucharist can be a renewal of the graces of baptism and confirmation. (We must note that the unity of the three sacraments does not preclude their being administered separately for pastoral reasons, for, as St. Thomas says, sacraments exist for the sake of us humans.)

Both the individual aspect of conversion and faith as well

as the ecclesial incorporation of baptism and confirmation are contained in the Eucharist. Hence, at Mass we are called to make an act of faith before communion, as well as to express reconciliation with each other at the sign of peace.

Our word *baptism* comes from the Greek *bapto,* which means "dip." And in its intensive form, *baptizo,* it means "to plunge" or "immerse." And the primary sign or element used in this sacrament is obviously water, to which we will now turn our attention as it is presented to us in the Bible.

Water in the Mystery of Redemption

Early in the Bible the Hebrew people made a literary borrowing from their Babylonian neighbors in whose mythology the sea (Tiamat) gave birth to the gods, only to be conquered by one of them. This conquest of the sea was the mythological counterpart for creation, since it amounted to bringing order out of the chaos of that "wild animal," the sea, that was so unpredictable when you mounted its back in a boat. The Hebrews "purified" the myth by attributing the powerful victory to the Lord.

In Psalm 104 we are told of the Creator's power over the waters of the sea—"At your rebuke they flee" (104:7), as would a cowering animal, taking flight and becoming subject.

In chapter 7 of Job the "creation" or control of chaos is not just an act of the past, but it calls for the continued vigilance and dominating power of the Lord. Similarly, in the first creation story in Genesis we are told that God's power separates the waters above and below the firmament so that humans may have a place for life.

The story of the crossing of the Red Sea in Exodus 14 is the Old Testament apex of God's continuing creative power or dominance over the animal, the sea. Recall that in the first story of God's covenant with Abraham, in Genesis 15, Abraham is instructed to split in two several animals as preparation for a covenant ceremony. But Abraham at this point is not asked to walk the path between the animals. Only the flaming torch, a symbol of God, goes through, for here God freely binds himself to Abraham—gives a free gift of covenant, or his "I choose never to be without you." The same kind of covenant ceremony takes place as the Hebrews walk through the split-open Red Sea in Exodus 14. So, in chapter 15, Moses and the men sing their canticle of thanksgiving, as the women dance in the same way they would at the celebration of a marriage covenant.

When Jesus calms the sea, in Mark 4, this literary classification of the sea shows up again as Jesus commands the chaotic sea to "silence," just as in chapter one Jesus rebuked the demoniac, saying, "Be quiet." The demoniac had reacted violently to the presence of Jesus, just as the sea did when Jesus mounted its back in a boat.

In the Book of Revelation we read that in the heavenly Jerusalem there will be no more sea, for God's victory over chaos and death will be complete (chapter 21).

All this imagery leads us up to Paul's crucial statement about baptism in Romans 6:3–5: "Do you not know that all of us who have been baptized into Christ Jesus were baptized into his death? Therefore we have been buried with him by baptism into death, so that, just as Christ was raised from the dead by the glory of the Father, so we too might walk in newness of life. For if we have been united with him in a death like his, we will certainly be united with him in a resurrection like his." Here Paul writes of the plunging into the chaotic waters of death as a burial in Christ's death. But just as in the crossing of the Red Sea, the "glory" of God brought the Hebrews through the waters of death alive, and at creation God's power separated the waters and held them back so humans could live, so did the "glory of the Father" raise Christ from the dead after he had been "baptized" with his passion and death ("the baptism that I am baptized with" [Mark 10:38]).

Paul concludes that when the Christian is brought out of the waters he or she shares in Christ's newness of life, and speaks of our death to sin in very absolute terms. Elsewhere, though, Paul recognizes that the Lord's victory is dynamic and still to be completed. At times this present and future tension in Paul has been expressed as an invitation to "become what you are."

While Paul chooses to use the imagery of the waters of death to explain baptism, the symbolic meanings of water are not limited to the "waters of death" or chaos. Water's symbolic meanings also include that of the "water of life." Ezekiel envisions the Jerusalem of the end-time with a stream of living water that flows from the temple to become deeper and deeper as a mighty river, and the Book of Revelation takes up the image again to describe the water of life flowing from under the throne of the new Jerusalem. And, as we know, John's Jesus tells us that he is the water of life, offering us eternal life. So often, then, the saving acts of the Lord in the Bible are described with this life-giving offer of water, just as at the crucifixion of Jesus "blood and water came out" of his side (John 19:34), very likely to refer to the Eucharist and baptism as Jesus' gifts to the church.

The life-giving aspect of water is found in our modern rite of baptism, when the minister says, "God the Father of our Lord Jesus Christ has freed you from sin, given you a new birth by water and the Holy Spirit, and welcomed you into his holy people."

For Reflection:

1. How does the Bible's imagery of the "waters of death" speak to our human experiences of chaos and need?

2. How does the Bible's imagery of the "water of life" speak to our human thirsts and experiences of God's gifts?

3. John's story of Jesus' death has already in it a sense of Jesus' victory. In that context, how does the "blood and water" flowing from his side relate to that victory?

Baptism in Early Christian Writers

We have considered baptism in the context of its roots in Scripture, but now we will turn to some of the early Christian writers for some insights from their beliefs and practices.

In the West the Apostles' Creed serves as what we might call the oldest Roman catechism to be used in the preparation of candidates for baptism. Of course, these doctrinal instructions were always accompanied by moral instructions and a careful look at the candidate's way of life.

The ceremony itself, preceded by prayer and fasting, began with a renunciation of Satan. Here, as in the other steps, bodily positions and gestures play an important role in the sacramentology of the rites. St. Cyril of Jerusalem tells us that the candidates would turn to the west and stretch out their hands in the direction of the west's darkness, saying, "I renounce you, Satan...I fear your power no more, for Christ has overthrown it." (In some of the rites the candidate even spits in the direction of the west to express very forcefully a contempt for all that Satan stands for as our adversary.) Then the renunciation of Satan was followed by an anointing of exorcism that today we refer to as the oil of catechumens. Then the candidate would turn to the east, the direction of light and what Christ has to offer, to make a profession of faith in each of the persons of the Trinity and in "one baptism for repentance." These ceremonies, St. Cyril tells us, took place in the "outer chamber," for not only were the bodily actions an important part of the ceremony, but the change of location likewise played an important role in this sacramentology until it led up to the eucharistic altar.

It is interesting that Cyril and other early fathers gave these explanations during Easter week, after the rites had been performed, for the rites were done in a very experiential way, and only later reflected on, much as we might reflect on what God has done for us in the sacraments.

After the profession of faith came the baptism itself, by three immersions into the baptismal waters, in the names of the divine persons. While immersion, with its relation to the word *baptism* was the usual manner of baptizing, the *Didache* in chapter 7 states: "Baptize as follows [with mention of the persons of the trinity], in running water....But if you have none, pour water on the head three times, in the name of the Father and of the Son and of the Holy Spirit."[1] So, even in the early days, infusion was a viable alternative to immersion.

Following the baptism, as the newly baptized persons came up out of the pool, a priest would anoint them with the "oil of thanksgiving" to represent their belonging to Christ,

---

1. *Didache*, chapter 7, cited by Johannes Quasten, *Patrology*, Vol. 1 (Utrecht-Antwerp: Spectrum Publishers, 1977), 36.

the Anointed One. (They went on to a second anointing by the bishop, what today we call confirmation, and received the kiss of peace before joining the community around the eucharistic altar.)

For Reflection:

1. How does the "bodiliness" of the early rites and their experiential nature relate them to our understanding of the incarnation?

2. As we reflect today on our own baptism, in what way can we come to appreciate better how this sacrament makes us special people in our relation to Christ and to each other?

CHAPTER TWO

Baptism's New Life, New Faith, and New Community

Baptized for a New Life

We return to Paul's passage on baptism in Romans 6:3–4: "Do you not know that all of us who have been baptized into Christ Jesus were baptized into his death? Therefore we have been buried with him by baptism into death, so that, just as Christ was raised from the dead by the glory of the Father, so we too might walk in newness of life."

This new life that is enabled by baptism and the other sacraments is a life of the Christian gospels. Each gospel begins its resurrection story with reference to an empty tomb where Jesus is not to be found, and from which the disciples are instructed to leave and go elsewhere to find Jesus. It is like a new exodus that leaves the tomb and the past behind. Then many of the gospel narratives relate how the risen Lord truly is not found in the past, but in the garden, along the road, in the upper room, along the seashore, and on the mountaintop. They speak vividly of how Jesus is found everywhere the disciples go. He is in their present and their future, just as he is in ours.

The gospel call to exodus, to leave the tomb behind, and to find Jesus in our present and future, parallels the personal journey of many Christians today. For some it is the tomb of fear they are called to leave in order to discover the authentic Christian wholeness characterized by Jesus' often-repeated invitation, "Do not be afraid." Their moralistic training and intimidating images of Jesus and the Father have become too crippling to allow them to recognize that our emotion of fear is meant to separate us only from what is truly a danger or threat. But the gospel Jesus can hardly fall into that category.

Others are called to leave behind the tomb of legalism they have come to identify as Christianity itself, for only too often legalism, as it did for the Pharisees, conceals from both ourselves and others our lack of trust and faith in Jesus as he is presented to us by the gospels.

Again, many of us find ourselves called to go forth from the tomb of seeking self-worth in achievements, or the very similar trap of living as people-pleasers. Deeper down, these can be read as the signs of unaffirmed persons, whereas the authentic experience and call of Jesus can lead us to find ourselves in him.

Likewise, in our collective Christian past, a tomb has been formed by spiritualities tainted by the antihuman influences of such schools and movements as Stoicism, Platonism, and Jansenism. The exodus from this tomb requires us to discern more carefully and recognize that the personal Creator of the human is most desirous of its fullness of life, both personal and communitarian.

In their invitation to exodus, the gospels speak to us of the liberating presence of the true Jesus. And they speak of him as the One who meets us on the road of our journey to lead us to the full humanness and the "new creation" joy of hearts afire at his risen presence, as were the hearts of the disciples who met him on their journey to Emmaus. Initially those disciples look sad and are deeply distressed, even surprised, at the "ignorance" of this stranger who joins them, as they express that formerly they had been hoping in Jesus. Then a subtle change takes place, one that leads them to urge Jesus to stay with them, and only later they reflect on the meaning of this change of heart to faith. The scene at Emmaus closes with their obvious joy as they hasten back to be witnesses to the community and seal their individual experiences in the common experience of the gift of peace, or wholeness, as the risen Lord appears to the group.

Each of these tombs has its isolating effect, but the gospel Jesus is always concerned with restoring those whom he heals to community, where they can share, celebrate, and embody what they have found in Jesus. And this Christian community is one that is called to recognize that its principal direction for growth is always characterized by faith, hope, and love—virtues that bind us together while at the same time they respect individual values and gifts.

For Reflection:

1. In what way is our exodus from these "tombs" something that is aided by the grace of baptism and the other sacraments?

2. In what way can our exodus also be an uphill struggle?

3. What insights and aids for our growth to new life can be helpful?

4. How can our relationship with Jesus be a very important factor for growth?

Profession of Apostolic Faith

The church felt the need for a good summary of the teachings of the apostles, and formulated what came to be known as the Apostles' Creed:

I believe in God, the Father almighty, creator of heaven and earth. I believe in Jesus Christ, his only Son, our Lord. He was conceived by the power of the Holy Spirit and born of the Virgin Mary. He suffered under Pontius Pilate, was crucified, died and was buried. He descended to the dead. On the third day he rose again. He ascended into heaven, and is seated at the right hand of the Father. He will come again to judge the living and the dead. I believe in the Holy Spirit, the holy catholic church, the communion of saints, the forgiveness of sins, the resurrection of the body, and life everlasting. Amen.

Its earliest form existed for sure in the second century. It included a belief in the Trinity, the church, and the forgiveness of sins. The more developed form, above, was used, as we have seen, in the Roman ceremony for baptism.

Often the Apostles' Creed is divided into three parts, as St. Irenaeus explains: "The first part speaks of the first divine Person and the wonderful work of creation; the next speaks of the second divine Person and the mystery of His redemption of men; the final part speaks of the third divine Person, the origin and source of our sanctification."[1] He adds that these

---

1. St. Irenaeus, *Adversus Haereses,* 1, 10, 1–2, cited by Johannes Quasten, *Patrology,* Vol. I (Utrecht-Antwerp: Spectrum Publishers, 1977), 300.

three parts are like three chapters of the "seal" that is given to us in baptism.

Saint Ambrose, on the other hand, tells us of a numbering of the parts of the Apostles' Creed as twelve, after the number of the apostles. He prefers this numbering because it reminds us of the fullness of the teachings of the apostles. Ambrose calls the Apostles' Creed "the Creed of the Roman Church, the See of Peter, the first of the apostles, to which he brought the common faith."[2]

Saint Cyril of Jerusalem cautions us that "this synthesis of faith was not made to accord with human opinions, but rather what was of the greatest importance was gathered from all the Scriptures, to present the one teaching of faith in its entirety."[3] Clearly he saw no tension or dichotomy between belief in Scripture and belief in this early Creed.

While we usually speak of the Creed as a "profession" of faith, in earlier times it was often thought of as a "confession" of faith. In the Bible the word *confession* is not only an admission of sins or faults, but more radically it refers to an act of thanksgiving for God's goodness. For example, Psalm 106 begins with the encouragement to "Praise the LORD! O give thanks to the LORD, for he is good; for his steadfast love endures for ever."

So, a "confession" of faith is an act of thanksgiving for God's revelation of the truths that save us and put us on the

2. St. Ambrose, *De Sacramentis*, II, 7, cited by Louis Bouyer, *Eucharist*, trans. Charles Quinn (Notre Dame, IN: University of Notre Dame Press, 1968), 238.

3. St. Cyril of Jerusalem, *Catechetical Instructions*, explained by Johannes Quasten, *Patrology*, Vol. I (Utrecht-Antwerp: Spectrum Publishers, 1977), with reference to F. J. Badcock, "The Apostles' Creed," in *The Church Quarterly Review*, 118 (1934).

path to fullness of life. In God, "truth" is his fidelity that calls us to a response of faith.

For Reflection:

1. How did the early church find this summary that we call the Apostles' Creed helpful and practical?

2. How does the promise of Jesus in John 8:32—"and you will know the truth, and the truth will make you free"—relate to the baptismal profession of faith?

Baptism of Infants

In Mark's Gospel, little children are brought to Jesus by their parents for a blessing, "and the disciples spoke sternly to them." Jesus' response was, "Let the little children come to me; do not stop them" (Mark 10:13–14). Some scholars tell us that "Come to me" was often used as an expression for baptism.

Likewise, in Acts 16:33, when Paul's jailer came to faith in the Lord Jesus, "he and his entire family were baptized." A household was not only the immediate family, but also the servants and their children. Very likely the jailer's household would have included small children.

On the more definite side, though, as early as the second century for what was probably the first time in patristic writings, Irenaeus mentions that because Christ came to save us, "through Him all are born again to God—infants, children, boys and youths, and old men."

We also have an early document called the *Apostolic Tradition* by Hippolytus of Rome that dates from around the year 215. In its description of baptism we find these instructions: "The little children are to be baptized first. If they can make an answer for themselves, they should do so. If not, their parents or some family member should answer for them."[4]

A contemporary of Hippolytus, Origen states that "the Church received from the apostles the tradition of also baptizing children."[5] Some of the early fathers preferred the eighth day, to parallel baptism with the Old Testament covenant of circumcision, but this was not very widespread.

We need to remember the story in Genesis 15 concerning God's first covenant with Abraham, in which God did not yet require a response from Abraham. If we look on the grace of God as truly a free gift, we can understand that God's gift of grace always precedes our response.

But on a very human level we can draw some parallels to infant baptism in the way we take care of infants. A mother speaks to her child, fondles it, and smiles at it, just as if the child could already understand all this. All the loving gestures of the mother are like an eager looking forward to the child's future response to the love that is lavished on it in so many ways. The baptism of an infant in "mother church" in a religious way has a real effect on the child that makes its eventual response possible. And when the child is brought up in a Christian milieu, the spiritual or religious development of the child leads warmly to its gradual understanding and acceptance or welcoming of its grace of baptism.

---

4. Hippolytus of Rome, *Apostolic Tradition*, Part 3, cited by Johannes Quasten, *Patrology*, Vol. II (Utrecht-Antwerp: Spectrum Publishers, 1977), 191.

5. Origen, *In Romanos Commentarium*, 5, 9, cited by Johannes Quasten, *Patrology*, Vol. II (Utrecht-Antwerp: Spectrum Publishers, 1977), 83.

For Reflection:

1. How does the gift of baptism lay the foundation for a child to respond to this gift with faith and love?

2. How does infant baptism highlight the importance of faith-sharing on the part of the parents, godparents, and the community?

The Communitarian Dimension of Baptism

In 1 Peter 2:5, we read that we are like "living stones" that God uses to make of us a "spiritual house." Frequently today churches place the baptismal font at the entrance of the church, symbolizing that this building, which is a sacramental of the church community, is entered by way of the baptismal font.

It would be artificial to separate our immersion into Christ from our "going into" the Christian community. We can notice even more clearly today the communitarian nature of this sacrament when not only parents and godparents are present, but often many family members and friends.

The Letter to the Ephesians lays clear stress on this communal nature of baptism when it tells us, "There is one body and one Spirit, just as you were called to the one hope of your calling, one Lord, one faith, one baptism, one God and Father of all, who is above all and through all and in all." (4:4–6).

In practice Roman Catholics recognize the validity of baptism in most other Christian communities, so that we have at least that degree of community or unity based on our common baptism. In recent years, when adults might wish to become Roman Catholics, they ordinarily are not given individual instruction, but gather as a community with sponsors for RCIA (the Rite of Christian Initiation for Adults) in local parishes. Those to be baptized usually have the sacrament administered to them in a community Easter Vigil ceremony, rather than alone.

We humans are social creatures, and the church emphasizes our social dimension constantly, especially in our reception of baptism and the other sacraments. As mentioned earlier, the church is named by many names, but foremost are the titles "people of God" and "body of Christ." God calls us as a people, and our membership in the body of Christ shows us clearly the linkage between our belonging to Christ and to each other in the Christian community.

For Reflection:

1. In what way can we understand baptism as a bond of unity among Christians?

2. Why would it be unnecessary to distinguish between our belonging to Christ and to each other as a result of our baptism?

CHAPTER THREE

Confirmation's Gift of the Pentecostal Spirit

Confirmation

As noted earlier, the three sacraments of initiation were often viewed as a continuous whole, climaxing in the Eucharist. And in the rites of the Eastern churches, the three are usually administered together. As our understanding and pastoral needs developed, some of the distinctions came to light. This development of differences might be compared to the difference between the gift of the Spirit in John, which takes place on Easter evening, and the more pedagogical approach of Luke that takes a step-by-step approach to Easter, Ascension, and Pentecost.

We note, though, that in John, when the risen Lord breathes his Spirit on the disciples, he relates this gift to mission: "I send you" (John 20:21), and especially to the mission of forgiving sins (John 20:23). Luke also relates the gift of the Spirit to mission, when in Acts Jesus says, "...and you will be my witnesses in Jerusalem, in all Judea and Samaria, and to the ends of the earth" (Acts 1:8). Just after the Pentecost gift of the Spirit in Acts, Luke tells us that they "began to speak in other languages, as the Spirit gave them ability" (Acts 2:4).

We can conclude from both Luke and John that confirmation, in addition to being often a more mature acceptance of the grace of baptism, is a special strengthening of the person within the church, a mission that varies according to the vocation of each confirmed person.

The ceremony of confirmation has two major elements, the laying on of hands and the anointing or "chrismation" of the recipient. And it is through these actions and their accompanying prayers that the gifts of the Spirit are bestowed.

For Reflection:

1. How do the different approaches of Luke and John help us understand the gradual development of confirmation as a distinct, though still related, sacrament?

The Gift of the Pentecostal Spirit

The word *Pentecost* comes from the Greek for "fifty days," because we celebrate the feast fifty days after Easter (see Acts 2:1–11). Before the liturgical reforms of Vatican II, Pentecost was almost like a separate feast, having its own octave, or eight-day celebration. But since those liturgical reforms, we are now called to look on Pentecost as the summit and solemn conclusion of the seven-week Easter celebration. Luke refers to the "day of Pentecost" (Acts 2:1) as a feast already in existence among the Jewish people, and as a fulfillment of something waited for. The Jewish people referred to this feast as the "Feast of [seven] Weeks." In the ancient way of counting, seven weeks were considered to be fifty days.

The Jewish Feast of Weeks was originally a harvest feast of thanksgiving fifty days after the feast of unleavened bread, or Passover. (The climate in Israel is very similar to that of southern Texas in which there often are two or three harvests.) As time went on, however, about two centuries before the time of Jesus the Feast of Weeks came to be celebrated more as a thanksgiving for the gift of the Torah (or "teaching law"), since the Jews considered the Law as a gift that could lead them to happiness. The covenant of this Law was concluded on Sinai, according to Exodus 19:1–6, fifty days after the departure from Egypt.

When Luke makes reference to Pentecost, he wishes to draw a parallel between Moses and Jesus. Just as Moses went up Mount Sinai into a cloud and received the gift of the Torah from God, Jesus also ascends in a cloud, receives the gift of the Spirit from his Father, and pours this gift out on the first Christians. And just as the Lord of Sinai came to make of Jerusalem his dwelling place, so it is also in Jerusalem, where Jesus died and rose, that the indwelling of the Spirit is given. (In Luke's Gospel there is an inward movement to the heart of religion, Jerusalem, and in Luke's Acts there is an outward movement from Jerusalem to bring Christianity to the world of the time.)

When in Acts, Luke adds that at Pentecost so many nations are represented—"every nation under heaven"—and yet they all understand the apostles in their own various languages, he is implying a reversal of the curse in the story of Babel where the people who tried to rival God in the tall tower have their language "scattered" so that they could not understand each other. Their sin is divisive, but at Pentecost the creative power of the Spirit heals their divisions. Only God with his creative power can bring about such healing and reconciliation.

Let us try to get something of a broader picture of Luke's theology of the Holy Spirit: In the Pentecost liturgy the Jews sometimes prayed Psalm 68: "Summon your might, O God;

show your strength, O God, as you have done for us before....[H]e sends out his voice, his mighty voice. Ascribe power to God, whose majesty is over Israel; and whose power is in the skies....[H]e gives power and strength to his people" (verses 28–35). In the same vein, Luke describes Pentecost as fulfilling the promise, "But you will receive power when the Holy Spirit has come upon you..." (Acts 1:8). And this community inaugurated by the Spirit finds in the Spirit its own law and covenant, again amidst an appearance of God and a manifestation of God's power (2:11–14), but also given again and again in Acts to believers.

In his Gospel, Luke tells us that when Jesus was about to choose the Twelve, he "went out to the mountain to pray; and he spent the night in prayer to God" (6:12). In Acts he paraphrases this by speaking of the apostles he had chosen "through the Holy Spirit" (1:2). These men were chosen to bring that gift of the Spirit to others, such as those listening to Peter's sermon when they were called to baptism (Acts 2:38). But there are also others who share this mission: the disciples, and eventually Paul.

The power of the Spirit is evidenced in so many ways in the community. Peter is filled with the Spirit when he speaks up before the Sanhedrin (Acts 7:55). The same is true of the missionary Barnabas, as well as Saul when the two are sent on mission. And the Christian community "had peace and was built up. Living in the fear of the Lord and in the comfort of the Holy Spirit, it increased in numbers" (Acts 9:31). And when the community is faced with a difficult decision about whether to impose the Mosaic law on Gentile converts, they make their decision in union with the Holy Spirit (Acts 15:18). Likewise presbyters elsewhere are given their charge of shepherding by the Holy Spirit (Acts 20:28).

When we put together Luke's theology of the Spirit in his two books, we cannot help but notice how extremely rich it is. Jesus, at his conception and through his ministry, is filled in an abiding and unique way with the Spirit. Then, when his paschal mystery is complete, a new age is ushered in, an age of salvation, and of the community whose inner and outer life is shaped by the presence and activity of the Spirit, so much so that we could say that the gift of the pentecostal Spirit defines the life of the community.

In First Corinthians, Paul was faced with a kind of self-centered competition that some of the Corinthians were engaged in, seemingly because of their gifts. Paul felt the need to clarify that the authentic gifts of the Spirit lead to unity and service. He lists some of the gifts: wisdom in speaking, the power to express knowledge, faith, the gift of healing and miraculous power, prophecy, discernment, tongues, and interpretations of tongues (1 Cor 12:8–11). But then Paul goes on to explain that the greatest gift of all is love, the kind that has the qualities of patience, kindness, lack of jealousy and pretense and snobbery. This love rejoices in truth (faithfulness); it trusts, hopes, and endures. Notice that these are all qualities found in the Jesus of the gospels.

John's Gospel points out that we need the inner speaking of the Holy Spirit if we are to understand the outer word of Jesus that we find in the gospels. In chapter 14 John recalls for us Jesus' promise that he will come back to us, after his glorification, in the gift of the Spirit. John then continues to explain, "On that day you will know that I am in my Father, and you in me, and I in you" (John 14:20). Through the Spirit's speaking in us, the words of Jesus become interiorized.

Before the gift of the Spirit, Jesus' words in some way remained outside the disciples, just as the words of the gospels might remain outside a person today. The outer word which we find in the gospels needs to be brought alive in the hearts of those who are attentive to it. This is the role of the Spirit who "teaches" and "reminds" us from within. And what the Spirit teaches and recalls are the words of Jesus—there is a correspondence between the inner word of the Spirit and the outer word of the gospels. Both need to go together, to cooperate. The outer word of the gospels in its own way helps us to hear better what the Spirit is speaking in our hearts, but the inner word vivifies the outer word so that its saving power is unleashed, and the "good news" can become effective in us.

For Reflection:

1. How is Pentecost, a story of God's new covenant in the Spirit, a story that offers us insight about the sacrament of confirmation?

2. Give some examples of how the Holy Spirit is so real or tangible in Luke's Gospel and Acts.

3. How can we apply the main ideas of Paul's teachings about the gift of the Spirit to our understanding of confirmation?

The Laying On of Hands

The earliest rite of confirmation was the laying on of hands, an action that has a rich background of meaning in the Bible. In Exodus 14:30 we are told that the Lord saved Israel on that day from the hand (power) of the Egyptians. The same meaning of power for "hand," or "handiwork," is expressed in Psalm 19:1: "The heavens are telling the glory of God; and the firmament proclaims his handiwork" (power). The hand can also symbolize the Spirit of God, as in 1 Kings 18:46, where Elijah was able to overcome the prophets of Baal because "the hand of the Lord" was on him. And Isaiah likewise could act powerfully in the Spirit because the hand of the Lord took hold of him (8:11).

The laying on of hands can also be a sign of blessing, as when Jacob laid his hands on his sons Ephraim and Manasseh to bless them (Gen 48:14), or when Jesus blessed the little children by placing "his hands on them" (Mark 10:16). And even beyond blessing, the laying on of hands can serve as an act of consecration, such as the time when the Lord instructs the Israelites to lay their hands on the Levites (Num 8:10), or when Moses laid his hands upon Joshua to ready him for his role of leadership.

Finally, the imposition of hands can be used as a sign of deliverance and cure, such as when Jesus laid hands on the stooped woman and "immediately she stood up straight and began praising God" (Luke 13:13).

For Reflection:

1. Why is it best not to limit the symbolic meanings of the laying on of hands to a single meaning with regard to confirmation?

2. How can these various meanings be related to the confirmation thrust of mission?

CHAPTER FOUR

The Anointed Faithful

Anointing with the Gift of Oil and the Gifts of the Spirit

As the understanding of confirmation developed, the even more expressive sign of anointing was included to show what God does for the Christian as found in Deuteronomy: "He will love you, bless you, and multiply you; he will bless the fruit of your womb and the fruit of your ground, your grain and your wine and your oil…" (7:13). Jeremiah picks up the same idea when he says that "they shall be radiant over the goodness of the LORD, over the grain, the wine, and the oil" (31:12).

The Holy Land in the time of the Bible, as now, was rich in olive trees, and an abundance of oil was a sign of salvation and eschatological happiness. Deuteronomy describes the promised land as full of "olive groves that you did not plant" (6:11). And when Hosea writes of the Lord's espousing his people in love and mercy, the Lord's promise includes "the grain, the wine, and the oil" (2:22). So consistent is this theme that Joel describes it in the context of the eschatological day of the Lord when the Lord promises: "I am sending you grain, wine, and oil, and you will be satisfied" (2:19).

To pour oil on someone's head amounted to wishing that person joy and happiness, while extending a sign of friendship and honor, as in Psalm 23:5–6, "You anoint my head with oil; my cup overflows. Surely goodness and mercy shall follow me all the days of my life." And again in Psalm 92:10, where the psalmist praises God because "you have poured over me fresh oil." The same theme is carried over into the New Testament when the woman at Bethany poured the perfumed oil on Jesus' head (Matt 26:7), and in the story of the penitent woman who anointed the feet of Jesus with perfumed oil (Luke 7:46).

The king and high priest are in a special way the "anointed ones," or the chosen and consecrated ones, and this divine choice is accompanied by the Spirit of the Lord's taking possession of them. In Zechariah 4:11–14 the prophet's vision includes fresh olive oil flowing through two channels to the two anointed ones of the Lord, the king and the high priest. And in the tenth chapter of Samuel, Samuel is instructed to anoint Saul, who is then told "the spirit of the LORD will possess you" (1 Sam 10:1–6).

The New Testament proclaims Jesus as the "Christ" or Anointed One par excellence because "God anointed Jesus of Nazareth with the Holy Spirit and with power" so that he would go about doing good works and healings...(Acts 10:38). Hebrews, too, describes Jesus with the words "therefore God, your God, has anointed you with the oil of gladness beyond your companions" (1:9).

The Christian shares in this anointing of Jesus. We can find this idea most vividly in a homily in 1 Peter to the "new born," a homily which contains all the basic themes of the initiation rites, such as the "spiritual sacrifices" and the "tasting of the goodness of the Lord," as well as the milk that later figures into the Easter rites of the *Apostolic Tradition*. While this homily does not specifically mention anointing, it nevertheless points to the results of our sharing in Jesus' anointing, and our Christian qualities of kingship, priesthood, and consecration (2:2–10).

The Fathers also explain baptism and confirmation as the "seal" of the Spirit. In the Old Testament a seal—such as that in a signet ring or a stamp—was a sign of authority (see Gen 41:42, where the Egyptian pharaoh gives Joseph such a ring). A seal is also a sign of ownership, and like a signature it was a promise or guarantee. This image of "seal" used by the Fathers for confirmation found its source in the New Testament, in which many passages refer to the Christian as marked by God's seal, and where frequently the seal is related to the gift or anointing of the Spirit, such as in Ephesians 1:13–14: "In him you also, when you had heard the word of truth, the gospel of your salvation, and had believed in him, were marked with the seal of the promised Holy Spirit; this is the pledge of our inheritance toward redemption as God's own people, to the praise of his glory." Notice that "sealed with the Holy Spirit" is in apposition with "pledge our inheritance." Here we come very close to having a definition of the seal of the Spirit as pledge. This seal of the Spirit received in confirmation is above all a confirming or strengthening with the gifts of the Spirit.

During the ceremony of confirmation, the bishop stretches out his hands over those to be confirmed, and prays: "Give them the spirit of wisdom and understanding, the spirit of right judgment and courage, the spirit of knowledge and reverence. Fill them with the spirit of wonder and awe in your presence."

The gifts of the Spirit are drawn from Isaiah (11:2), where the prophet speaks of the qualities the Lord would give to the Davidic kings. Unfortunately those kings did not live up to these gifts. In his Easter instructions on the sacraments, St. Ambrose named each of the gifts and related them to the spiritual seal that is conferred in confirmation.

At whatever age confirmation is received, there is always an adult quality to its effects. Wisdom, or the ability to discern what truly leads to happiness, and courage to face up to frequent challenges enable the Christian to live in a countercultural way, to live gospel values in a society that might fall short of these values. Here again the gifts received individually can thrive best with the support of the church community.

While the gifts of the Spirit have a personal effect in the one being confirmed, and in a sense complete the gifts of baptism, they nevertheless have a missionary orientation. They offer the one confirmed the wisdom, understanding, and courage to witness to the faith both in that person's virtuous way of life as well as in his or her way of reaching out to others with the charity that Paul insisted is always the chief gift of the Spirit.

For Reflection:

1. Explain how our anointing puts us into relationship with Jesus, the Anointed One who went about doing good.

2. What qualities of oil and anointing in the Bible carry over into the rich meaning of confirmation?

3. Explain the biblical meaning of "seal" as it applies to confirmation.

4. How do the confirmation gifts of the Spirit relate to the challenges we face in society?

The Priesthood of the Anointed Faithful

The faithful who are anointed in baptism and confirmation share in the priestly anointing of our High Priest, Jesus. We are a priestly people, in a manner that is like our sharing in his Sonship and his sacrifice. For we too are invited to take up his cross (Matt 16:24) and to drink of his cup (Matt 20:22).

Paul looks on the faith of Christians as a "sacrifice" and an "offering" (Phil 2:17), and for him acts of charity are an offering pleasing to God (Phil 4:18). His understanding is very explicit when he asks the Romans to "by the mercies of God, present your bodies [their very selves] as a living sacrifice, holy and acceptable to God, which is your spiritual worship" (Rom 12:1).

The First Letter of Peter states that Christians are "a chosen race, a royal priesthood, a holy nation, God's own people, in order that you may proclaim the mighty acts of him who called you out of darkness into his marvelous light" (2:9). These phrases hearken back to the words the Lord spoke to his messenger Moses on Sinai. The gist of these titles is clearly one of privilege and blessing that calls for a "liturgy" of praise and thanksgiving.

In the Old Testament the prophets told Israel of its duty to respond to these blessings by sharing the word and worship of the true God with the nations. The same task is taken up by Christians, but now with the help of Jesus and the gift of his Spirit.

Holding primacy in our "spiritual sacrifice" is love, as we find in Ephesians: "...live in love, as Christ loved us and gave himself up for us, a fragrant offering and sacrifice to God" (5:2). At the very essence of the sacrifice of Jesus and Christians is the self-giving of love.

The priesthood of the faithful is a broad concept within which the sacrament of holy orders, of course, holds a related, yet in some ways distinct, role. The ordained priesthood, however, has as its primary activity to serve the up-building of the priesthood of all the believers who are sealed by God's Spirit.

The Vatican II document on the church offers an insightful summary of the blessing we call the priesthood of the faithful: "The baptized, by regeneration and the anointing of the Holy Spirit, are consecrated to be a spiritual house and a holy priesthood, that through all the works of Christians they may offer spiritual sacrifices and proclaim the perfection of him who has called them out of darkness into his marvelous light. Therefore all the disciples of Christ, persevering in prayer and praising God, should present themselves as a sacrifice, living, holy and pleasing to God" (2:10).

For Reflection:

1. How is the priesthood of the faithful based on a living communion with Christ that is given to us through baptism and confirmation?

2. How does our sharing in the priesthood of Christ give a special value to our efforts to live out our call to a life of faith and love?

CHAPTER FIVE

Eucharistic Spirituality and the Gifts of Bread and Wine

The Sacrament of Thanksgiving

The word *eucharist* comes from the Greek word for thanksgiving. Saint Paul tells us that the pagan religions of his time did not "give thanks to him [God]" (Rom 1:21), and extensive historical studies prove his statement to be true.

Very often we say that the major contribution of Judaism is belief in one God. And yet that important contribution of Judaism goes beyond its belief in *one* God—it adds another very important dimension, that this God is the kind of God to which we owe thanksgiving.

Many of the pagan religions of Abraham's time believed their gods wanted the sacrifice of the first-born son, but Abraham's God intervened to prevent Abraham from sacrificing Isaac (Gen 22), for he is not the kind of God who takes delight in human sacrifice. He is the loving and faithful God who bound himself in covenant to Abraham. So Abraham had to be taught that God's saving will is by nature above the whimsical demands of the neighboring pagan gods. And so much more about God's saving and gracious will would be revealed later in the central event of the Pentateuch, the exodus.

We can easily contrast a liturgy of thanksgiving that expresses our gratitude for what God has given us, from a liturgy offered to appease an angry god. The key to the contrast is what kind of God we believe in. Yes, we do have our sins and faults to be sorry about, but our sins are not powerful enough to change God's loving nature. Or as we read in 1 John 3:20: "...we will know that we are from the truth and will reassure our hearts before him whenever our hearts condemn us; for God is greater than our hearts, and he knows everything."

In biblical language, "to praise God," "to bless God," and "to thank God" all have the same meaning. And the Bible shows a marked preference for liturgies of thanksgiving. We can read, for example, of a disdain for the old forms of animal sacrifice in Psalm 50:13–14, "Do I eat the flesh of bulls, or drink the blood of goats? Offer to God a sacrifice of thanksgiving, and pay your vows to the Most High."

For Reflection:

1. How can we allow our own attitudes to be shaped most of all by a quality of thanksgiving in our prayers, whether we are alone or with others?

2. What role does memory play in the development of thanksgiving?

3. What might be obstacles to a quality of thanksgiving in our prayers and liturgies?

The Gift of Bread

The biblical background on the gift of bread supplies a wealth of meaning for our Christian Eucharist.

Let us begin with the story of the manna in Exodus 16. In verses 17 to 30 we find detailed instructions for the people about the gathering of the manna: they are told to gather enough for one day only, and if they gather more, they find that worms infest the manna; and yet when the Sabbath is coming, they are told to collect enough for two days. Hesitant as they are, they collect for two days, and it works out fine— no worms. As Deuteronomy and Jesus would say, we do not live by bread alone, but by following God's word. Bread and God's word or instructions must go hand in hand. So in Exodus the Sabbath rest is a sign of confidence in God, showing that we do not live by our own labors but by God's gift.

In Deuteronomy 8 the theme continues by pointing out that the gift of manna was a test to humble the people and to bring them to realize that even after their liberation in the exodus they were still dependent on God, and that they must possess God's gifts *as gifts*, not as some kind of personal property.

When we come to Proverbs 9 we read about the bread (and wine) in the context of a banquet, or food for wisdom, wisdom being understood as a practical form of knowledge that leads to happiness, life, and the Lord's favor.

Further insight is gained in Isaiah 55:10–11, "For as the rain and the snow come down from heaven, and do not return there until they have watered the earth, making it bring forth and sprout, giving seed to the sower and bread to the eater, so shall my word be that goes out from my mouth; it shall not return to me empty, but it shall accomplish that which I purpose, and succeed in the thing for which I sent it." Notice there is a circular motion of God's gifts that come forth from God and return to God bearing fruit, a fruit of thanksgiving (called "fruit on the lips" in the Bible). In this line of thought, bread and thanksgiving are linked together as results of God's blessings.

One of the best-known teachings on bread, of course, is found in chapter 6 of John. The structure of the chapter is the story of the multiplication of the loaves at Passover,

Jesus' walking on the sea that recalls the exodus story of crossing the sea, and the discourse on the bread of life. The first part of the discourse stresses faith in God's Word (see John 1:1), Jesus himself, who is the gift of bread, or God's teaching, God's wisdom come down from heaven, for this belief in God's Word leads to eternal life, a gift far surpassing the manna in the desert. Then Jesus goes on to explain that this bread of life is his flesh, the Eucharist, which is clearly related to the incarnation of the Word.

In verse 56 of John 6, we find a key notion for John: "Those who eat my flesh and drink my blood abide in me, and I in them." This "remaining" in Jesus is for all practical purposes John's definition of a disciple. By contrast, in verse 66, we are told that the teaching and gift of Jesus are just too much for some, so that they would not "remain in his company any longer." But for the disciple there is a mutual indwelling; the disciple remains in Jesus and Jesus remains in the disciple, for Jesus, as the bread of life, is an interiorization of the gift of covenant, God's choosing to be with us in the gift of Jesus, God's Word and Bread.

For Reflection on the Gift of Bread:

1. Explain the relation between the bread of the manna and God's Word or instructions.

2. How does the Eucharist express a mutual indwelling or "remaining" between the disciple and Jesus?

The Gift of Wine

In Jewish liturgical tradition wine was referred to as "the fruit of the vine." And in the Bible we find a rather consistent theme of the vine as a symbol of the chosen people.

Chapter 5 of Isaiah begins with a vineyard song, telling the story of a farmer sparing no effort to build a vineyard, only to be disappointed by its poor production of grapes. Then the meaning of the story is explained in verse 7: "For the vineyard of the LORD of hosts is the house of Israel."

In the prophet Ezekiel, chapter 15, we find the theme again in a parable of the vine. The wood of the vine cannot be used for any purpose but to bear good fruit, for its wood is too brittle for other uses. The lesson is that God's people need to keep faith and bring forth the fruit God wants from them.

Mark, in chapter 12, takes up the theme of a man planting a vineyard, leasing it out to tenants, only to be dismayed at how the tenants do not want to share the fruit of the vine with him—another story of disappointment with how God's people act.

While John's Gospel does not describe the institution of the Eucharist at the Last Supper, it does use the symbolism of the bread of life in chapter 6 and the allegory of the vine in the discourse of Jesus at the Last Supper. There Jesus explains, "I am the vine, you are the branches" (John 15:5). Here again we find the Johannine theme of the mutual indwelling the disciples share with Jesus, who is our source of life. Jesus is the true vine, and his blood is the drink of the new covenant. This could be a new emphasis in the biblical theme of the vine, namely that the vine is life-giving.

There is a very ancient eucharistic prayer in a document called the *Didache* (teachings) that includes a prayer of thanks to the Father "for the holy vine of David." We cannot overlook the fact that when Jesus calls himself the bread of life and the true vine, he is giving us a revelation of who Jesus is for us as our savior. A few times in John the words "I am" stand alone, expressing the divine identity of Jesus.

But when "I am" is used with expressions such as "bread of life," "light of the world," "gate of the sheep," or "good shepherd," John is trying to help us understand who Jesus is *for us*, a role that requires many metaphors to give us even a glimpse of all that Jesus is as savior. (We can add as an afterthought that the wine used at the time of Jesus was very strong and even syrupy, so that it was usually mixed with some water. See for example the mention of mixing wine in Proverbs 9:5.)

For Reflection on the Gift of Wine:

1. The notion of covenant is a binding of people together for a sharing of life. The ancients looked on blood as the place of life in us—so covenant ceremonies often made use of a sprinkling of blood. How does the Eucharist carry out this understanding of covenant?

2. How does the allegory of the vine in chapter 15 of John stress this notion of life in common?

CHAPTER SIX

Roots of Eucharistic Spirituality in the Passover and in Christian Writers

The Passover Meal

The exodus liberation is the apex of the meaning of redemption in the Hebrew Scriptures. In the twelfth chapter of Exodus, no doubt written under a later liturgical influence, the Passover meal is described and ordered for the night before the exodus redemption or liberation, and this meal with the lamb and unleavened bread in many ways is a sign-meal that in advance would give meaning to the Lord's redemptive activity in the exodus of the next day. The ritual of marking the doors with blood so the people would be spared and freed the next day is also such a sign.

The words of the father of the family in a Jewish Passover meal pronounced down through the centuries over the various foods, conferred on them a power to evoke the past and inspire a hope for the future, as well as a power to personalize the saving activity of the exodus—"*I* was a slave in Egypt and the Lord freed me."

The theme of thanksgiving is uppermost: "Blessed are you, O Lord our God, king of the universe, for the fruit of the vine," a praise or thanksgiving prayer repeated over the food at each of the three parts of the meal, and then again at the conclusion, the psalms of "alleluia" and the "alleluia" (or "praise God") cup. And before the main course, with its breaking of the bread and cup of thanksgiving, there is always a *haggadah*, or narration, of God's wonderful deeds.

The Synoptic Gospels picture the Last Supper of Jesus and his disciples as just such a Passover meal (see Matt 26:17–19). Jesus' words of institution of the Eucharist would fit in with the breaking and thanks for the bread—"This is my body"—and with the cup of thanksgiving—"This is my blood"—during the main course of the meal. But it is important to note also that the Synoptics place this Last Supper on the night before Jesus' redemptive death in order to clarify the meaning of his death.

To all appearances, Jesus is betrayed or handed over by one of his disciples. But the institution of the Eucharist tells us that we must look deeper to understand the true reality. This Last Supper shows us that in fact with the gift of the Eucharist Jesus is not being passively "handed over," rather that *he is handing himself over* in the eucharistic bread and wine. Just as the Passover meal in Exodus interprets in advance the meaning of God's saving of his people, so this Last Supper brings home to us how Jesus goes voluntarily to his death to accomplish God's saving plan. And ultimately Jesus passes over from death to life to bring this salvation to its fulfillment.

For Reflection:

1. How does God's freeing of his people offer us a good understanding of what redemption means?

2. What importance do the Synoptics put on the personally free nature of Jesus' death as seen in the gift of the Eucharist?

An Early Christian Eucharistic Prayer

The *Didache* (teachings of the Twelve Apostles) is a short work in Greek from early in the second century, probably of a Syrian-Palestinian origin. It was discovered in 1875 in Constantinople. Chapters 9 and 10 of this work contain instructions for eucharistic rites that form a kind of missing link between the Jewish meal prayers and the early Christian eucharistic prayers.

In chapter 9 we read, "About the Eucharist, give thanks in this way: First over the cup—We give you thanks, our Father, for the Holy Vine of David your Servant Jesus. Glory to you forever! Amen. Then about the breaking (of the bread): We give you thanks, Our Father, for the life and knowledge You have revealed to us through your Servant Jesus. Glory to you forever! Amen. Just as this broken bread was all around the hills and then gathered together into one loaf, so may your Church be gathered from all the earth into your kingdom. For to you belong the glory and the power forever through Jesus Christ."

Then in chapter 10 we find these instructions: "After you have been filled with food, give thanks in this way: We give thanks to you, O Holy Father, for your holy name (presence), which you have made to dwell in our hearts, and for the knowledge, faith and immortality which you have revealed to us through your Servant Jesus. Glory to you forever! Almighty Lord, you have created all things for your name's sake. You gave food and drink to men for their enjoyment, so that they may give thanks to you. But you have blessed us with spiritual food and drink, and with eternal life through your Servant. So we give thanks to you above all because you are mighty. Glory to you forever. Lord, remember your community and deliver it from all evil, and bring it to perfection in your love, and gather it from the four winds, as it has been made holy, into your kingdom that you have prepared for it. For yours is the power and the glory forever."

We can notice in these ceremonies and prayers a parallel between the first cup of the Passover meal, as well as the first cup in Luke 21:17 (a cup that has puzzled some who have not related it to the seder), with the first cup in chapter 9 of the *Didache*. The similar parallels between the Passover's breaking of the bread, Jesus' taking of the bread in Luke, and the breaking of the bread in the *Didache* also come to our notice. The same is true of the final thanksgiving cup in all three sources.

Within these parallel structures there is an emphasis in the *Didache* on knowledge (*gnosis*). In Paul's writings, *gnosis* refers to the discovery of a hidden meaning of Scripture as seen only in Christ. So the sense is that God has revealed to us the mystery or inner reality of the Vine of David through the sending of his Servant-Son. And this *gnosis* or revelation becomes experiential, tangible, for us in the sacrament of thanksgiving.

When, in this sacrament, God "makes his name [presence] dwell in our hearts," we recall the Old Testament notion of *shekinah*, or the presence of God with his people. The *Didache* points out to us that just as the rabbis spoke of the *shekinah* in the midst of those participating in a religious meal, so for Christians the incarnation and the Eucharist are the revealed modes of God's presence with us. The *Didache*, then, stresses the continuity between the two Testaments.

For Reflection:

1. How does the *Didache* offer us insight about the continuity of the two Testaments?

2. How are we to understand our Christian *gnosis* today?

The Real Presence of the Risen Lord

In the Letter to the Ephesians we are told that the glorified Christ is a fullness "of him who fills the universe in all its parts." The Eucharist is our sacrament or visible sign of this real presence.

From the earliest times of the church there has been a firm belief in the real presence of Christ in the Eucharist. Around the turn of the first century the martyr Ignatius of Antioch was critical of a group that denied the human nature of Jesus, and so Ignatius wrote: "From Eucharist and prayer they hold aloof: because they do not confess that the Eucharist is the Flesh of our Savior Jesus Christ, which suffered for our sins, and which the Father in His loving-kindness raised from the dead." And in another letter that he wrote on his way to martyrdom in Rome he added: "Take care, then, to partake of one Eucharist; for one is the flesh of our Lord Jesus Christ, and one the cup to unite us with His blood."

Clement of Alexandria, born about the year 150 AD, continued in the same line of thought. Commenting on John 5:53, he says, "Eat my flesh and drink my blood. Such is the suitable food which the Lord ministers....O amazing mystery!"[1] In the fourth century Basil the Great refers to receiving the Eucharist

---

1. Clement of Alexandria, *Paedagogus*, 2, 2, cited by Johannes Quasten, *Patrology*, Vol. II (Utrecht-Antwerp: Spectrum Publishers, 1977), 30.

as a partaking of the "holy body and blood of Christ."[2] In the West, Saints Ambrose and Augustine offer us numerous passages that leave no doubt about their belief in the real presence of Jesus in the Eucharist.

When we come to St. Thomas Aquinas, in the thirteenth century, we find a philosophical-theological attempt to explain what is involved in the transformation of the bread and wine into the body and blood of Christ. Thomas used the term *transubstantiation*. He said that while the "accidents" of bread and wine remain the same, the "substance" changes.[3] By "accidents" he means all the perceptible or visible qualities of bread and wine, and that these do not change in the celebration of the Eucharist. But the "substance," or deeper and imperceptible reality, does change, so that the relationship that the accidents had to their substance is changed into a relationship of these accidents to the risen body of Christ. And since that relationship is a real one, and not just one in our minds, the presence of the risen body of Christ is a real presence.

Three centuries later, when the Council of Trent defined the real presence, it came very close to the explanation of Thomas, but instead of the word *accidents* it used the word *species* as a deliberate effort to show not only respect for Thomas, but also to show that the explanation of Thomas is not the only valid explanation.

Some explanations are clearer than others, but this belief of the church in the eucharistic real presence stems from the New Testament, especially a passage such as the

2. Basil the Great, *Ep. 93*, cited by Johannes Quasten, *Patrology*, Vol. III (Utrecht-Antwerp: Spectrum Publishers, 1977), 233.
3. St. Thomas Aquinas, *Summa Theologica*, Tertia Pars, q. 75, art. 2 (Madrid: *Biblioteca de autores cristianos*, 1964). Author's translation.

one in 1 Corinthians 10:16: "The cup of blessing that we bless, is it not a sharing in the blood of Christ? The bread that we break, is it not a sharing in the body of Christ?"

Perhaps our best personal and communal approach to the mystery of the real presence of the risen Lord can be found in St. Thomas' words from his hymn for Corpus Christi, "Let faith supply what is lacking to our senses." And, of course, let our faith be the faith of the church.

For Reflection:

1. Is there some benefit in trying to understand in some degree what we mean by the real presence of Christ in the Eucharist, even though we can never fully grasp it in this life?

2. If faith in the Eucharist is a gift, what does it mean to call faith something that goes beyond our powers to understand?

The Eucharist and the Holy Spirit

The Letter of Paul to Titus makes a connection between baptism and the Holy Spirit when it talks about God's saving us through "the water of rebirth and renewal by the Holy Spirit" (3:5).

When Luke tells us of the conception of Jesus, the angel says to Mary in 1:35: "The Holy Spirit will come upon you, and the power of the Most High will overshadow you..."("Holy Spirit" and "power of the Most High" are stated as parallels with the same meaning). The main thrust of Luke's message is that Jesus' incarnation is a gift that only God could give us, a gift from God's Holy Spirit.

From this background developed the two invocations of the Holy Spirit in our eucharistic prayers: The first invocation, in prayer two, reads: "Let your Spirit come upon these gifts to make them holy, so that they may become for us the body and blood of our Lord Jesus Christ." This invocation is asking for the transformation of the bread and wine into the sacrament of the Eucharist. The second invocation says: "May all of us who share in the body and blood of Christ be brought together in unity by the Holy Spirit." We can refer to this second invocation as a "fruits" invocation, for it asks that the grace of communion be effective in us, especially in bringing about our union with Jesus and with each other— a blessing of the end-time to a degree advanced to us in the sacrament.

So, this relation of the Eucharist and the Holy Spirit brings out two main ideas: the "gift" nature of the Eucharist—it is all God's doing—and its relation to the incarnation, when Mary was overshadowed by the Holy Spirit in order to bring into existence the body and blood of Jesus now present in the Eucharist.

For Reflection:

1. God's power comes to us in the activity of the Holy Spirit. Often power can be something that frightens us. What is different about the power of the Holy Spirit so that we need not fear it?

2. How do the two invocations of the Holy Spirit in eucharistic prayer two make it clear how dependent we are on God in a continuous way as we celebrate the Eucharist?

CHAPTER SEVEN

The Blessings of the Eucharist

Eucharistic Forgiveness

In Matthew's narration of the institution of the Eucharist, we read, "for this is my blood of the covenant, which is poured out for many for the forgiveness of sins" (26:28). And, close to Matthew's account, in our Mass we use the words: "Take this all of you and drink from it, for this is my blood, the blood of the new and everlasting covenant, which will be shed for you and for all so that sins may be forgiven."

With these texts in mind, St. Thomas Aquinas, in a work about the feast of Corpus Christi, wrote: "No other sacrament has greater healing power; through it sins are purged away, virtues are increased and the soul is enriched with an abundance of every spiritual gift."

In the same vein, when the priest gives communion to the deacon, in the divine liturgy of the Byzantine rite, the priest says: "Receive the blood of Christ for the forgiveness of your sins."

We can understand this notion of forgiveness better when we consider the initiation rites of the early church: baptism, confirmation, and Eucharist. There was a unity in the progression of these rites, so that the forgiveness of sins granted in baptism reached its climax in the reception of the

Eucharist, just as the same progression from one sacrament to another ritualized the person's movement toward the very center of the church, Christ himself. The progression was dramatized in the progression from baptistery to altar.

Of course, we do not wish to belittle the forgiving power of the sacrament of reconciliation—sometimes we have a real need to "tell the doctor where it hurts!" But let us recall the quote from St. Thomas above. He equates the purging away of sins with the healing power of the Eucharist. This equation invites us to look more carefully at what sin is, so that we can have a better grasp of eucharistic forgiveness.

The prophet Jeremiah (7:18–19) claims that the sinner intends to hurt God, but that the sinner misses the mark and ends up hurting himself or herself instead. The prophet's insight respects the transcendence of God and points out that the results of sin are harmful to the sinner and others. He does not picture God as indifferent, however, but rather as a God who wishes to use his creative power to bring about a remedy for human sinners. Jeremiah and other Old Testament writers try to put our focus on the extent of God's love for us. God forbids sin because humans will be hurt by it. That is why the Old Testament word for God's Law is *Torah*, or "teaching," because God's law is a gift that teaches us about God's love and about the kind of lifestyle that will not only help us avoid harm but even lead us to an insight about what can make us happy.

Our English word *sin* also tells us a lot about the meaning of sin, and is derived from the German word *sunde* from which we get our English word *asunder*. Sin, whether we notice it or not, splits us off from our deepest good, and at times also from others. Sin, therefore, is an alienation from the good in ourselves and in others. The opposite of this alienation is a reconciliation within ourselves and with others—think, for example, of the "sign of peace" before communion.

Yet the old nursery rhyme about "Humpty Dumpty" gives us a real insight about reconciliation. Recall that, after Humpty's fall, all the king's horses and men—all human efforts—were unable to put Humpty together again. Such a healing from our alienation calls for God's creative activity.

That is where we find further understanding from Psalm 51 ("Have mercy on me, O God..."). This psalm uses words for God's merciful activity such as "cleanse," "wash," and above all "create." In the Old Testament "to create" is used to describe the initial creation of the world, the liberation of the Hebrews from Egypt, and ultimately God's creation of a *new* heaven and earth, or his putting all together again as a *new* creation.

In his Second Letter to the Corinthians, chapter 5, Paul explains that just as in the Old Testament rituals of at-one-ment (*yom kippur*) or reconciliation, the sprinkled blood of life joins God and his people in covenant, so Jesus' crucifixion and resurrection make of us "a *new* creation" (5:17).

We conclude then that when Matthew describes Jesus as giving his "blood of the covenant," Matthew calls on the meaning of covenant, which perhaps can best be translated as God's gift of choosing never to be without us. Matthew describes us as having a "communion" in Jesus' Passover from death to life.

Our focus on the Eucharist as forgiveness, then, does not allow us to stop at the miracle of the real presence, but leads us forward to the miracle of God's creative act of reconciliation that he offers us in the Eucharist.

When at Mass the priest calls us to behold "the Lamb of God who takes away the sins of the world," he is calling us to have a grateful faith by which we open our hearts to the gift of Jesus, who in this paschal sacrament is personally our gift of forgiveness and new life.

For Reflection:

1. What do we mean when we say sin is an alienation within ourselves, a splitting us off from our own deepest good? And also at times an alienation between ourselves and others?

2. What is there about the celebration of the Eucharist that can heal our interior and exterior divisions?

A Twofold Remembering

Jesus' words at the Last Supper in Luke, "Do this in memory of me," when taken in the context of their biblical background, have a two-fold meaning with reference to *our* remembering and *God's* remembering.

Psalm 78:7, for example, tells us that God's people "should set their hope in God, and not forget the works of God, but keep his commandments." Here we see that remembering God's deeds is closely related to hope, and to a moral life. We remember God's deeds because through his actions on our behalf he reveals his own nature of loving kindness, which invites our response of hope and gratitude (Eucharist), and of living in accord with his commands.

When we turn to Psalm 136, a hymn of thanksgiving (again, Eucharist), we find a narration of God's deeds: his making of the heavens, the earth, the lights, all creation in verses 1 to 9, and a narration of redemption, the exodus, in verses 10 and following. His deeds are narrated for us to remember, that is, to personalize or interiorize their meaning. And we also notice that this psalm is in the form of a litany, with the people's constant response of "his mercy endures forever."

In Psalm 105:1–5, we find again a narration of God's deeds in the context of giving thanks to the Lord or seeking his face, which is another way of inviting us to remember and personalize the "wonderful works he has done." (Later, in verse 8, there is mention of God's remembering of his covenant, the aspect of God's remembering that we will consider in the second part of our reflections.)

The aspect of our remembering Jesus in the celebration of the Eucharist is meant to draw us and our lifestyle closer to him—to take him within us (as opposed to the fearful response of hiding from God as Adam and Eve did after their sin), and to live with the kind of love that Jesus exemplified for us.

The German theologian Joachim Jeremias has pointed out that Jesus' words to "do this in memory of me" have a second meaning drawn from the Hebrew Scriptures and liturgical practice. He tells us that there is an effective or causal side that the Bible refers to as God's remembering. When in Luke 1:72, in Zechariah's priestly canticle, we read that God "has shown the mercy promised to our ancestors, and has remembered his holy covenant"—a thought we saw earlier in Psalm 105—Zechariah is referring to God's memory as an effective and creative fulfillment of what God has promised.

In the Hebrew Scriptures there is a word for such a memorial, *Zikkaron*, something that is brought into the sight of God to "remind" him. The shewbread in the temple is such a "reminder" before God, or placed in God's sight. The twelve jewels on the high priest's vestment also are worn into the sight of the Lord to beg his mercy on the twelve tribes of Israel. (Some other examples of this usage are found especially in Exodus and Leviticus.)

If the celebration of the Eucharist is understood in the second way, God's remembering, then the words of Jesus in Luke would mean "Do this so that God may remember me." It recalls the third benediction or prayer of thanks of an old Passover prayer which asks God to remember "the Messiah, son of David your servant....May this remembrance come before you for rescue, for goodness."

Paul's words in 1 Corinthians 11:26 explain that "For as often as you eat this bread and drink the cup, you proclaim [to the Father] the Lord's death until [can also be understood as 'so that'] he comes."

As we have seen, in *our* remembering we recall the past event of the Lord's death and resurrection, but in *God's* remembering we look on Jesus' death as the beginning of salvation time. In the celebration of the Eucharist we place the body and blood of the Lord in the sight of the Father so that through the priesthood of Christ the Father is urged to bring about what is still unfulfilled in our salvation, namely the second coming of the Lord. The Eucharist is a plea for the Father to send Jesus. It is the prayer of *maranatha* for the Lord's second coming.

This idea is implied in the eucharistic prayer of the Swiss Reformed community: "We place, O God, in the presence of your divine majesty this bread and wine" as a sacrifice of praise, and "on the basis of the promise of his return we wait for the day when he will come in power and glory." Likewise, we are familiar with how in the Roman Catholic eucharistic prayers we so often ask God to "remember" his people, both living and departed, so that God's saving power will be bestowed on us through the priesthood of the risen Lord.

Finally, let us add that when Luke narrates the Last Supper, including the words "Do this in memory of me," he uses a word of purpose (*eis* in Greek, or "so that") with reference to the remembering. He is indicating that Jesus commands us to celebrate the Eucharist "so that" we may personalize and interiorize what Jesus has done for us (our remembering), and also "so that" the Father will send his Son in the second coming to bring about the fulfillment of God's saving plan for us (God's remembering).

For Reflection:

1. How are God's deeds in both Testaments acts of revelation or teachings for us about God himself? Explain the effects our remembering of God's deeds can have on us.

2. What is the connection between God's "remembering" and the completion of our redemption?

The Sacrament of the Resurrection

We are told by John that "Those who eat my flesh and drink my blood have eternal life, and I will raise them up on the last day" (6:54).

For John, the narration of Lazarus coming out of the tomb when Jesus called him forth is like a picture of our final resurrection: "Very truly, I tell you, the hour is coming, and is now here, when the dead will hear the voice of the Son of God, and those who hear will live" (John 5:25).

And while John's community faced problems and doubts in the face of those who did not "remain" as disciples, the Eucharist is a real "presence" of the One who seemed absent. The Eucharist is a "Presence" but most of all it is a power for hope and resurrection.

Over many centuries the liturgy for the second Sunday of Easter, which contains the gospel resurrection appearance to "doubting Thomas," has caught the spirit of this story in the communion antiphon sung as the faithful would hold out their hands to receive the Eucharist: "Stretch out your hand and know the place of the nails." This account in John concludes in the upper room where the Last Supper had been celebrated with an explanation that these stories of Jesus "...are written so that you may come to believe that Jesus is the Messiah, the Son of God, and that through believing you may have life in his name" (John 20:31). This without doubt is the life promised in the eucharistic passage on "eternal life" in chapter 6.

Paul too stresses the paschal nature of our Christian life as our way of sharing in the life of the risen Lord. The resurrection of Christ, the center of Paul's preaching, is oriented toward his glorious second coming (1 Cor 15:22ff), and it is in this context that Paul understands the Eucharist.

Something of the life given us in the Eucharist and the other sacraments is an anticipation of our final glory of resurrection, for which we are called to have a sure and joyous hope. Paul's confidence can be seen in his metaphor of the "first fruits of the Spirit" that he used to describe God's saving action in us (Rom 8:23). First fruits can be tasted, experienced, in the present, as a guarantee of a fuller harvest to come.

For Reflection:

1. While the Eucharist leads us to eternal life, what does it mean for us to say that this resurrection can in a degree be advanced to us today on our journey, through the grace of the Eucharist?

2. What needs in our own life would we most like Jesus to "raise up" by the power of the sacrament working through our receptive faith?

CHAPTER EIGHT

The Sacraments in Our Faith Lives

Baptism and the Eucharist

There is a traditional axiom about the sacraments that they cause what they signify. In other words, the visible sign illustrates for us the meaning of the interior grace the sacrament confers.

Baptism, we believe, is a gift of new life, of rising with Christ out of the "waters of death" into the risen life of Jesus, as well as a reception of the gift bestowed by the "waters of life"—both biblical images complementing each other to express the new birth found in the sacrament.

Then the Eucharist, with its signs of food and drink, nourishes the new life of baptism in us. It helps us continue to grow in both our personal spiritual life as well as in our living out of the bonds of unity and love in our church community. And when we look at the element of forgiveness in the Eucharist, we see again how the Eucharist fosters our growth in the grace of baptism.

In practice, then, we can say that the Eucharist is like a renewal of the grace of our baptism, as well as a nourishing that helps our life in Christ continue to grow. And since baptism (as well as confirmation) points to our reception of the Eucharist, we can say that in some way the Eucharist is the goal and even in a way a defining feature of baptism, since a goal gives meaning to the steps along the way to the goal.

For Reflection:

1. How can we understand baptism and the Eucharist as related to each other through their connection with our new life in Christ?

2. In what way can we say that the Eucharist can be a renewal of our grace of baptism?

Baptism, Confirmation, and Eucharist in Our Daily Lives

The English poet, Rudyard Kipling, wrote that he longed to go to "where there ain't no ten commandments." An attitude like this, whether or not it was truly Kipling's attitude, misses entirely the biblical approach to *Torah*, the law, or more literally, "practical teaching," as a gift meant to lead us to happiness. For example, the ten commandments in essence teach us that our lives, even here on earth, will not be happy if they include such things as killing, lying, stealing, and the like.

The same is true of the new law of Jesus as we find it, for example, in Matthew's Sermon on the Mount in chapters 5 through 7, with the Beatitudes and other instructions on anger, retaliation, the Golden Rule, and so on. This sermon lays out a beautiful plan for daily life in the community Jesus is founding, since it comes right after the call of the first disciples in chapter 4.

But what we particularly need to notice is the enlightening way Matthew locates this Christian law of life in such a way that it is followed immediately by a series of miracles: the healing of the leper, the cures of the centurion's servant, of Peter's mother-in-law, the calming of the storm, the expul-sion of demons, the cures of the paralytic and the woman with a hemorrhage, the raising of the little girl whom he took by the hand so gently, the cures of the two blind men, and the cure of the possessed mute.

This very arrangement of stories shows us that Matthew wants to tell us that not only does Jesus teach a new way of life based on love, but that he goes beyond his teaching to put his curing, capacitating, and life-giving power into our lives. This is Jesus' way of taking us by our hand and lead-ing us along the path of his gift of the law of life.

The sacraments offer us today this same enabling presence of Jesus. The graces or gifts given to us in the sacraments can be paralleled with the acts of power we see in the gospel stories of Jesus' cures and giving of new life. Through the continued presence and power of Jesus in the gifts of the sacraments, we today can approach his teachings on a real beatitude or happi-ness in our lives. His gifts of teaching in the New Testament are accompanied for us today with sacramental power to live his teachings. No doubt we still need to put our own efforts into being poor in spirit, forgiving, and loving our enemies, and liv-ing with the kindness and goodness Jesus modeled for us. But the gift of his power in the sacraments accompanies the gift of his word. And in this very practical way in our daily lives we can experience how word and sacrament go together, just as they usually do in our celebrations of the sacraments. Our efforts and Jesus' power form a unity in our daily lives.

For Reflection:

1. Contrast the different understandings of God's law as gift or as burden.

2. How does Matthew arrange his gospel stories to show us how Jesus' teachings for life and his miracles go hand in hand?

3. How can the teachings of Jesus and the power of the sacraments form a unity in our daily lives?

The Sacraments of Faith

Faith is a word with many different facets of meaning. At times there is an emphasis on creedal faith, as, for example, a belief in the truths expressed in the Apostles' Creed, as we saw earlier regarding the profession of faith in the Roman baptismal ritual. Another principal aspect of faith is that of confidence or trust, an attitude that goes beyond an intellectual assent to truths.

Nevertheless it is important for us to recognize that in the New Testament these two aspects of faith are far from being in opposition to each other. For example, a belief in the truth of God's being almighty and merciful can be a powerful reason for trusting in him. And when, in Matthew 16, after Peter had seen the power of Jesus' miracles, he speaks for the other disciples the truth about Jesus: "You are the Messiah" (16:16). Peter here expresses a personal and trusting union with Jesus, along with an insight about Jesus that forges a greater union among the disciples also.

Another aspect of faith is its acceptance and even active welcoming of God's plan. When Joseph had scruples about Mary before the birth of Jesus, the angel told him: "Have no fear about taking Mary as your wife." Matthew's Greek word for *taking* is a form of *lambano*, which implies this accepting and welcoming of God's will. This dimension of faith combines a person's belief about God and trust in God with a willingness to obey God. Mary, like Joseph, is such a listening and obedient person. Paul refers to this as "the obedience of faith" (Rom 1:5) and believing "with the heart" (Rom 10:10).

We believe in the sacraments as experiential signs and effective channels of God's grace. At the heart of this faith is a personal and prayerful relationship of faith with the Lord. For this reason the sacraments are, except in extreme emergencies, celebrated along with a liturgy of the word in order to foster a prayerful and essential faith relationship with the Lord.

At the core of both liturgical and personal prayer is an awareness of God's presence and an awareness of our personal relationship with God rather than ritual practices alone. For this requirement of true prayer the Bible has much to tell us.

As we look into the Old Testament, especially in its earlier stages, we find many symbols and images used to convey something of the experience of God's presence. One such representation is the holy place, an example of which is found in the story of Abraham's call and his subsequent journey to the holy place of Shechem: "Abram passed through the land to the place at Shechem, to the oak of Moreh. At that time the Canaanites were in the land. Then the LORD appeared to Abram, and said, 'To your offspring I will give this land.' So he built there an altar to the LORD, who had appeared to him" (Gen 12:6–7).

For ancient men to leave home and break ancestral bonds was nearly unthinkable. Yet Abraham had done it. Something of a personal intervention and presence is already represented in his migration, and as he goes, one Canaanite holy place after another seems to reaffirm the reality of the presence of the One who called. The altar he builds becomes a sign of this reality, at first silent and non-combative in the regions of other gods, and yet tremendously significant of the reality of the One who called.

As worship was eventually localized in one central sanctuary, the religious experience could be well expressed in a prayer attributed to Solomon:"...that your eyes may be open night and day toward this house, the place of which you said, 'My name shall be there,' that you may heed the prayer that your servant prays toward this place" (1 Kgs 8:29). The sanctuary then was a symbol of God's faithful love in the gift of his presence.

But even Solomon is portrayed as being conscious that the holy place is inadequate to express all of what God's gift of himself comprises when his prayer is qualified with the words, "Even heaven and the highest heaven cannot contain you, much less this house that I have built!" (1 Kgs 8:27). Solomon's qualifying statement eventually grows to John's statement about worship in spirit and truth (4:21). Such historical progress from temple to all-present Spirit finds its counterpart in a microcosmic way in the growth of an individual person to an awareness of God's presence in an all-pervading way, as seen in St. Teresa of Avila's experience of a constant immersion in God.

A second symbol in the Bible of the Lord's presence is the Lord's face, a more personalized way of speaking of this presence. Let us try to understand what religious experience this human yet reverent imagery conveys. We read that "...the LORD used to speak to Moses face to face, as one speaks to a friend" (Exod 33:11). But when Moses voices his fear about moving on from the place where they had been camping, the Lord assures him that "My presence will go with you, and I will give you rest" (Exod 33:14). Later, while instructing the people, Moses reminds them that the Lord brought them out of Egypt. He openly showed his face and his great power (Deut 4:37). And we cannot overlook the priestly blessing that contains the words asking the Lord to let his face shine on the people and be gracious to them (Num 6:25).

The story of Moses likewise informs us that when Moses went to the meeting tent, "the pillar of cloud would descend and stand at the entrance of the tent, and the LORD would speak with Moses" (Exod 33:9). Or as the people began their wilderness march, "The LORD went in front of them in a pillar of cloud by day, to lead them along the way" (Exod 13:21). There seems to be a certain tension here in the cloud imagery—the tension of an "already" and "not yet" about the presence of the God who speaks and guides, for the cloud gives a visible sign of his presence at the same time that it veils him.

We are reminded of the same tension found in contrasting passages in *The Spiritual Canticle* of John of the Cross: "It is noteworthy that, however elevated God's communication and the experiences of His presence are, and however sublime a person's knowledge of Him may be, these are not God essentially, nor are they comparable to Him because, indeed, He is still hidden to the soul."[1] Yet the same John later adds: "O, then, soul, most beautiful among all creatures, so anxious to know the dwelling place of your Beloved that you may go in quest of Him and be united with Him, now we are telling you that you yourself are His dwelling and His secret chamber and hiding place. This is something of immense gladness for you, to see that all your good and hope is so close to you as to be within you."[2]

---

1. *Spiritual Canticle,* stanza 1, par. 3.
2. Ibid., par. 7.

One of the high points of Old Testament insights about God's presence is its quality of enduring in spite of adverse human circumstances; but it took the suffering of the exile to bring that high point into view. The exiles, surely, typify those in adverse conditions, those for whom God's presence seems unlikely if not impossible. Yet it is especially to them that the promises of Isaiah are addressed: "When you pass through the waters, I will be with you; and through the rivers, they shall not overwhelm you; when you walk through fire you shall not be burned, and the flame shall not consume you. For I am the LORD your God, the Holy One of Israel, your Savior" (Isa 43:2–3).

While those in adverse circumstances might be far from experiencing God's presence, the prophet here calls them to a faith in the reality of his enduring presence. In fact, he seems to claim that those going through the waters and fire are in a special way the recipients of the promise. It is similar to the message found in Romans when Paul asks, "Who will separate us from the love of Christ?" (8:35). And the promise in Isaiah is guaranteed with "I am the Lord your God," where the focus is taken off our circumstances and placed on God. The gift of his presence is not dependent on us but on him. Even our faults and weaknesses are taken up into God's love and the grace of his presence. Realizing and confessing that we cannot be worthy of his presence frees us to know he is close.

Psalm 139 is an excellent example of how God leads us to an expanded awareness of his presence, an awareness that is reaching out to grasp at the reality of a personal presence beyond locale:

> Where can I go from your spirit?
> Or where can I flee from your presence?

If I ascend to heaven, you are there;
if I make my bed in Sheol, you are there.
If I take the wings of the morning
and settle at the farthest limits of the sea,
even there your hand shall lead me,
and your right hand shall hold me fast.

(Ps 139:7–10)

But the secret of such an awareness lies in a shift of perspective from our efforts to know God's presence to the ways he chooses to make us present to him—something like the shift that takes place in the story of a lover who runs after the beloved until the beloved catches the lover.

In a maturing religious experience, God's activity becomes more central to the experience than ours. We come to know that his thinking of us and loving us are the means by which he raises our minds and hearts to his presence, his means of communicating his presence to us on this deeply personal level, as he does in the sacraments.

The incarnation and the sacraments that flow from the incarnation add such a different dimension to God's presence. While it is true that in Old Testament times God did not hesitate to use somewhat inadequate human symbols and experiences to reveal his presence, in the incarnation the mystery of a personal union that is not transitory brings God's self-communication into the realm of the human as only the unique relation of this mystery to the eternal procession of the Word could (see Heb 1:1–3).

Matthew's Gospel begins with the news of the Emmanuel to remind us that even with the limitations of Jesus' earthly life, his disciples experienced in him as never before the presence of God, so that even about his earthly life they could later reflect on "what was from the beginning, what we have heard, what we have seen with our eyes, what we have looked at and touched with our hands" (1 John 1:1).

But Matthew's Gospel goes on to refer us to the Paschal exaltation of Jesus in which the limitations of time and space are surpassed in his very humanity and a Lordship is given in which the risen Christ can be present at every point of the universe. And so the Emmanuel theme of the first chapter is more than matched by the gospel's final promise, "And remember, I am with you always, to the end of the age" (Matt 28:20). Consequently, in each gospel narrative of the resurrection events, there is the underlying theme of a discovery of Christ's living presence. A faith of the heart in his resurrection is then for us, too, a belief and an assurance of his presence.

Essentially both liturgical prayer and personal prayer are that moment in which through God's help we are able to focus on him instead of ourselves. This kind of personal awareness or personal relationship with the Lord is what can change our reception of the sacraments from some kind of mechanical ritual to a truly grace-filled event. And the sacramental moments can in a much fuller way be experiential and effective signs teaching us about the gift of the presence of the Lord in this life until we reach the fullness of the beatific or face-to-face vision that the sacraments of faith can lead us to.

For Reflection:

1. How is a holy place a symbol of God's presence in the Bible?

2. The Bible uses "cloud" as a symbol of God's presence. A cloud can be a visible sign, but it also can veil things from us. What might this tell us about the Lord's presence with us in the sacraments?

3. What strikes you most about the prayer regarding God's presence in Psalm 139?

4. How do the sacraments serve as signs of Jesus' covenant promise to be with us always?